NURSERY RHYMES

Illustrated by David Crossley

Brown Watson
ENGLAND

HICKORY, DICKORY DOCK

Hickory, dickory dock,
The mouse ran up the clock.
The clock struck one,
The mouse ran down,
Hickory, dickory dock.

LITTLE JACK HORNER

Little Jack Horner sat in a corner,
Eating his Christmas pie;
He put in his thumb,
And pulled out a plum,
And said "What a good boy am I!"

THREE BLIND MICE

Three blind mice, three blind mice,
See how they run, see how they run!
They all ran after the farmer's wife,

Who cut off their tails
With the carving knife,
Did you ever see
Such a thing in your life,
As three blind mice?

OLD MOTHER HUBBARD

Old Mother Hubbard
Went to the cupboard,
To get her poor doggy a bone.

But when she got there,
The cupboard was bare,
And so the poor doggy had none!

MARY HAD A LITTLE LAMB

Mary had a little lamb,
Its fleece was white as snow,
And everywhere that Mary went
That lamb was sure to go.

It followed her to school one day,
That was against the rule;
It made the children laugh and play,
To see a lamb at school.

JACK BE NIMBLE

Jack be nimble,
Jack be quick,
Jack jump over
The candlestick.

THIS LITTLE PIGGY

This little piggy went to market,
This little piggy stayed at home,
This little piggy had roast beef,
This little piggy had none.
And this little piggy cried,
"Wee, wee, wee," all the way home!

THERE WAS A CROOKED MAN

There was a crooked man,
And he walked a crooked mile,
He found a crooked sixpence
Against a crooked stile;

He bought a crooked cat,
Which caught a crooked mouse,
And they all lived together
In a little crooked house.

THE GRAND OLD DUKE OF YORK

Oh, the grand old Duke of York,
He had ten thousand men;

He marched them up to the top of the hill,
And he marched them down again.
And when they were up, they were up,
And when they were down, they were down,
And when they were only halfway up,
They were neither up nor down.

SOLOMON GRUNDY

Solomon Grundy,
Born on a Monday,
Christened on Tuesday,
Married on Wednesday,
Took ill on Thursday,

Worse on Friday,
Died on Saturday,
Buried on Sunday,
And that was the end
Of Solomon Grundy.

ONE, TWO, BUCKLE MY SHOE

One, two, buckle my shoe;
Three, four, knock at the door;
Five, six, pick up sticks;
Seven, eight, lay them straight;

Nine, ten, my fat hen;

Eleven, twelve,
dig and delve.

LUCY LOCKET

Lucy Locket lost her pocket,
Kitty Fisher found it.
Not a penny was there in it
But a ribbon 'round it.

DOCTOR FELL

I do not like thee, Doctor Fell,
The reason why I cannot tell;
But this I know, I know right well
I do not like thee Doctor Fell.

TWEEDLEDUM
AND TWEEDLEDEE

Tweedledum and Tweedledee
Agreed to fight a battle,
For Tweedledum said Tweedledee
Had spoiled his nice new rattle.

Just then flew by a monstrous crow,
As black as a tar barrel,
Which frightened both the heroes so,
They quite forgot their battle.

I'M A LITTLE TEAPOT

I'm a little teapot,
Short and stout,
Here's my handle,
Here's my spout.

When I see the teacups,
Hear me shout:
Tip me up and pour me out!

BOBBY SHAFTO

Bobby Shafto's gone to sea,
Silver buckles on his knee;
He'll come back and marry me,
Bonny Bobby Shafto.

Bobby Shafto's bright and fair,
Combing down his yellow hair;
He's my love forever more,
Bonny Bobby Shafto!

ROUND AND ROUND THE GARDEN

Round and round the garden
Like a teddy bear.
One step, two steps,
Tickle me under there.